THIS BOOK BELONGS TO

_____

13-Digit ISBN: 978-1604337808
10-Digit ISBN: 160433780X

This book may be ordered by mail from the publisher. Please include $5.99 for postage and handling. Please support your local bookseller first!
Books published by Cider Mill Press Book Publishers are available at special discounts for bulk purchases in the United States by corporations, institutions, and other organizations. For more information, please contact the publisher.

Cider Mill Press Book Publishers
"Where good books are ready for press"
PO Box 454
12 Spring Street
Kennebunkport, Maine 04046
Visit us online!
cidermillpress.com

Typography: Georgia, Trajan, and Voluta Script Pro
Image Credits: Democratic Presidential candidate Hillary Clinton speaks to a crowd (Krista Kennell / Shutterstock.com); Signature of Hillary Rodham Clinton (Wikimedia Commons); The house in Park Ridge, IL where Hillary Rodham Clinton grew up (vnews.tv / Shutterstock.com); First Lady Hillary Rodham Clinton (Library of Congress Prints and Photographs Division LC-DIGds-00125); President Bill Clinton and First Lady Hillary Clinton with young Kosovar refugees near Skopje, Macedonia (Wikimedia Commons); First Lady Hillary Clinton at a Congressional hearing on health care reform (Library of Congress Prints and Photographs Division LC-RC15-1993-690); President Barack Obama and Secretary of State Hillary Clinton at the East Asia Summit (Wikimedia Commons); The Clintons with daughter Chelsea (Wikimedia Commons); Hillary Clinton on the Clinton-Gore 1992 presidential campaign (Joseph Sohm/ Shutterstock.com); Democratic presidential candidate Hillary Clinton at a campaign event (Joseph Sohm/ Shutterstock.com); President Bill Clinton and First Lady Hillary Clinton dancing at the first inaugural ball (Library of Congress Prints and Photographs Division LC-USZC4-5394); First Lady Hillary Clinton at a Congressional hearing on health care reform (Library of Congress Prints and Photographs Division LC-RC15-1993-690) First Lady Hillary Clinton greets U.S. troops in Bosnia (Wikimedia Commons); Democratic presidential candidate Hillary Clinton and First Lady Michelle Obama at a campaign event (Joseph Sohm/ Shutterstock.com); Portrait of Hillary Clinton (courtesy of the Clinton Foundation); The First Lady with First Cat Socks and First Dog Buddy (Wikimedia Commons); First Lady Hillary Clinton speaking at the United Nations 4th World Conference (Wikimedia Commons); Hillary Clinton speaks from the podium at a campaign event (Evan El-Amin / Shutterstock.com); Original home owned by Bill and Hillary Clinton in Little Rock, AR (Joseph Sohm/ Shutterstock.com)

Printed in China
1 2 3 4 5 6 7 8 9 0
First Edition

HILLARY RODHAM CLINTON

NOTEBOOK

CIDER MILL PRESS

BOOK
PUBLISHERS
KENNEBUNKPORT, MAINE

Introduction

BY MIM HARRISON, AUTHOR OF MINI-BIOGRAPHIES
OF FIRST LADIES JACQUELINE KENNEDY AND
ELEANOR ROOSEVELT

*W*hen Hillary Diane Rodham was a high school student in the early 1960s, she decided to run for class president. Just what made her think, demanded a male opponent, that a *girl* could get elected?

She lost that race, but never the determination to succeed. Her CV, which might well still be a work-in-progress, is replete with accomplishments that few can top—not even her fellow graduates of Yale Law School.

She was First Lady of Arkansas for four terms, beginning in 1978, when her husband, Bill, was the state's governor. Then she was First Lady of the United States, from 1993 to 2001. From there she smoothly segued into being elected—twice—a United States Senator from New York State. That made her America's first First Lady to ever win a public office. And from 2009 to 2013, she served as President Barack Obama's Secretary of State.

Three years later, Hillary became the first American woman to run for president with the endorsement of a major political party. Thanks to this historic moment, references to a Clinton presidential campaign now need to distinguish between which Clinton, Bill or Hillary.

You might say that, from the day she was born (October 26, 1947, in Chicago), Hillary was always a go-getter. Not surprisingly, so were her very first heroines.

The first was Jo March, the fictitious protagonist of *Little Women*, and the sister in the story that Hillary most closely identified with out of the four. Years later, Hillary told her interviewer for *Oprah* Magazine that *Little Women* was "one of the first literary explorations of how women balance the demands of their daily lives."

Her other childhood heroine was also a fictitious character, a young woman for whom words like "roadster" and "sleuth" came easily: Nancy Drew. The fact is, Hillary Rodham Clinton is an inveterate reader, and usually reads every night before turning in. As she told an audience of librarians not long after she lost her presidential bid in 2016, she found solace in returning to "the familiar experience of losing myself in books."

And, according to her husband, there are many opportunities to do so in their home in Chappaqua, New York. He happily lamented to guests at the 2017 National Book Awards dinner that books were in overabundance in their household. Some of those are no doubt the books that Hillary herself has written, including *It Takes a Village: And Other Lessons Children Teach* (1996), *Living History* (2003), *Hard Choices* (2014), and *What Happened* (2017).

It's said that Hillary has kept a list of every book she's read as an adult. That would make the list not only long but eclectic—novels, history, biography, commentary, even poetry. In the latter category, Mary Oliver and Maya Angelou are two favorites; Angelou read her poem, "On the Pulse of Morning," for Bill Clinton's first presidential inauguration, in 1993.

Among the many books on Hillary's list will be *The Brothers Karamazov, The Signature of All Things,* and *The Color Purple.* And she still has a soft spot for mysteries, especially those by Louise Penny, Donna Leon, and Jacqueline Winspear.

Another book that Hillary has pointed to as a favorite is *West with the Night*, Beryl Markham's autobiographical account of her solo flight across the Atlantic, flying east to west. She was the first aviator to achieve this.

Another go-getter—this one real, rather than fictitious. Much like Hillary Rodham Clinton.

Our founders fought a revolution and wrote a Constitution so America would never be a nation where one person had all the power. Two hundred and forty years later, we still

PUT OUR FAITH IN EACH OTHER.

—Speech at the 2016 Democratic National Convention in Philadelphia, Pennsylvania, accepting the Democratic nomination for President of the United States (July 28, 2016)

Passing on the gift of
freedom and the

OPPORTUNITY

that comes with being an
American may be our most
important obligation.

*—Remarks highlighting the Charter of Freedoms Project, National
Archives Rotunda, Washington, DC (July 1, 1999)*

President Bill Clinton and First Lady Hillary Clinton hold hands with young Kosovar refugees in at a camp near Skopje, Macedonia (June 22, 1999)

We have the responsibility to create a society in which we expand the benefits of

DEMOCRACY AND FREEDOM

to all of our fellow citizens; where we ensure that free markets benefit all people, not just a privileged few; where we create and nurture vibrant civil societies that foster active citizens.

—Remarks on globalization delivered at the Sorbonne, Paris, France (June 17, 1999)

Every woman deserves the chance to

REALIZE HER OWN GOD-GIVEN POTENTIAL.

But we must recognize that women will never gain full dignity until their human rights are respected and protected.

—*Remarks at the U.N. Fourth World Conference on Women in Beijing, China* (September 5, 1995)

First Lady Hillary Clinton at a Congressional hearing on health care reform (September 1993)

That is our duty, to build that
bright future, and to teach our
children that in America there is no
chasm too deep, no barrier
too great – and no ceiling
too high – for all who

WORK HARD, NEVER BACK DOWN, ALWAYS KEEP GOING,

have faith in God, in our country,
and in each other.

*—Speech at the 2008 Democratic National Convention in Denver,
Colorado (August 26, 2008)*

President Barack Obama and Secretary of State Hillary Clinton at the East Asia Summit at the Peace Palace in Phnom Penh, Cambodia (November 20, 2012)

I want to speak up for mothers who are fighting for good schools, safe neighborhoods, clean air, and clean airwaves; for older women, some of them widows, who find that, after raising their families, their skills and life experiences are not valued in the marketplace; for women who are working all night as nurses, hotel clerks, or fast food chefs so that they can be at home during the day with their children; and

FOR WOMEN EVERYWHERE

who simply don't have time to do everything they are called upon to do each and every day.

—Remarks at the U.N. Fourth World Conference on Women in Beijing, China (September 5, 1995)

There should be no exceptions, no excuses, to our solemn commitment that every child can learn; every child deserves to be challenged, to have their

IMAGINATIONS SPARKED.

—Acceptance speech for the Friend of Education Award Presentation to the First Lady, Orlando, Florida (July 5, 1999)

The Clintons with daughter Chelsea (1993)

IMAGINE A TOMORROW WHERE NO BARRIERS HOLD YOU BACK, AND ALL OF OUR PEOPLE CAN SHARE IN THE PROMISE OF AMERICA.

Imagine a tomorrow where every parent can find a good job and every grandparent can enjoy a secure retirement, where no child grows up in the shadow of discrimination or under the specter of deportation, where hard work is honored, families are supported, and communities are strong, a tomorrow where we trust and respect each other despite our differences, because we're going to make positive differences in people's lives.

—*Speech after winning the New York Democratic Primary for presidential candidate, New York City* (April 16, 2016)

None of us can raise a family, build a business, heal a community, or lift a country totally alone.

AMERICA NEEDS EVERY ONE OF US

to lend our energy, our talents, our ambition to making our nation better and stronger.

—Speech at the 2016 Democratic National Convention in Philadelphia, Pennsylvania, accepting the Democratic nomination for President of the United States (July 28, 2016)

Hillary Clinton on the Clinton-Gore 1992 presidential campaign in Corsicana, Texas (August 28, 1992)

The potential within every person to learn, discover, and embrace the world around them, the potential to

JOIN FREELY WITH OTHERS TO SHAPE THEIR COMMUNITIES AND THEIR SOCIETIES

so that every person can find fulfillment and self-sufficiency, the potential to share life's beauties and tragedies, laughter and tears with the people we love – that potential is sacred.

—Remarks on the Human Rights Agenda for the 21st Century at Georgetown University, Washington, DC (December 14, 2009)

Every time a barrier to progress has fallen, it has taken a

COOPERATIVE EFFORT

from those on both sides of the barrier.

—*Speech at the U.N. Human Rights Council headquarters in Geneva, Switzerland* (December 6, 2011)

*President Bill Clinton and First Lady Hillary Clinton
dancing at the first inaugural ball in Washington, DC
(January 20, 1993)*

What we are learning around the world is that if women are healthy and educated,

THEIR FAMILIES WILL FLOURISH.

If women are free from violence, their families will flourish.

If women have a chance to work and earn as full and equal partners in society, their families will flourish.

—Remarks at the U.N. Fourth World Conference on Women in Beijing, China (September 5, 1995)

People should be free
from tyranny in whatever form,
and they should also be

FREE TO
SEIZE THE
OPPORTUNITIES
OF A FULL LIFE.

—Remarks on the Human Rights Agenda for the 21st Century
at Georgetown University, Washington, DC
(December 14, 2009)

First Lady Hillary Clinton at a Congressional hearing on health care reform (September 1993)

Everywhere I travel, I meet people not just looking to us, but asking us for leadership. This is a source of strength, a point of pride, and a great opportunity.

BUT IT IS AN ACHIEVEMENT, NOT A BIRTHRIGHT.

—Remarks at the 2011 U.S. Global Leadership Coalition Conference, Washington, DC (July 12, 2011)

I often use a very simple metaphor to talk about society—that of a three-legged stool: one leg is the government, another is the economy, and the third is a civil society....We need three legs that balance and reinforce one another, and that are

STRONG

enough to support us in the years to come.

—Remarks on globalization delivered at the Sorbonne, Paris, France (June 17, 1999)

First Lady Hillary Clinton greets U.S. troops in Bosnia
(December 22, 1997)

When there are
no ceilings,

THE SKY'S
THE LIMIT.

—*Speech at the 2016 Democratic
National Convention in Philadelphia,
Pennsylvania, accepting the Democratic
nomination for President of the United
States (July 28, 2016)*

Democratic presidential candidate Hillary Clinton and First Lady Michelle Obama at a campaign event in Winston-Salem, North Carolina (October 27, 2016)

Where do human rights begin? In small places, close to home, so close and so small that they cannot be seen on any maps of the world....Such are the places where every man, woman, and child seeks

EQUAL JUSTICE, EQUAL OPPORTUNITY, EQUAL DIGNITY

without discrimination.

—Remarks to the U.N. Economic and Social Council on the 50th anniversary of the Universal Declaration of Human Rights, New York City (December 10, 1997)

When any barrier falls in America,
it clears the way for

EVERYONE.

*—Speech at the 2016 Democratic National Convention in
Philadelphia, Pennsylvania, accepting the Democratic nomination
for President of the United States (July 28, 2016)*

Portrait of Hillary Clinton

To fulfill their potential, people must be free to choose laws and leaders; to share and access information, to speak, criticize, and debate.

THEY MUST BE FREE TO WORSHIP, ASSOCIATE, AND TO LOVE IN THE WAY THAT THEY CHOOSE.

And they must be free to pursue the dignity that comes with self-improvement and self-reliance....

—Remarks on the Human Rights Agenda for the 21st Century at Georgetown University, Washington, DC (December 14, 2009)

The First Lady with First Cat Socks and First Dog Buddy
(April 7, 1999)

KNOCKING DOWN BARRIERS

means we can't just talk about economic inequality, we also have to take on racial inequality.

—Ohio Democratic Party Legacy Dinner, Columbus, Ohio
(March 13, 2016)

First Lady Hillary Clinton speaking at the United Nations
Fourth World Conference on Women in Beijing, China
(September 5, 1995)

Women must enjoy the rights to participate fully in the social and political lives of their countries, if we want

FREEDOM AND DEMOCRACY

to thrive and endure.

—Remarks at the U.N. Fourth World Conference on Women in Beijing, China (September 5, 1995)

About Cider Mill Press
Book Publishers

Good ideas ripen with time. From seed to harvest,
Cider Mill Press brings fine reading, information,
and entertainment together between the covers
of its creatively crafted books. Our Cider Mill
bears fruit twice a year, publishing a new crop
of titles each spring and fall.

"Where Good Books Are Ready for Press"

Visit us on the Web at
www.cidermillpress.com
or write to us at
PO Box 454
12 Spring St.
Kennebunkport, Maine 04046